Library of Congress Catal
Copyright © 1974 by The Phi De
Blooming

TABLE OF CONTENTS

INTRODUCTION

"Oh, if I could only bundle it all up and take it home with me!" This was the exclamation of delight from a first-year teacher who was spending a day visiting a well-functioning informal classroom. Her joy could be understood as one scanned the room appreciating the variety of learning activities underway.

On one side of the room were two small plastic wading pools joined by a piece of plastic pipe. In them, the children had set up a habitat for about a dozen large frogs and toads, using big pieces of turf and stones in one pool and keeping tadpoles at various stages of growth in the other. The children talked intelligently about the habitat, how life within it functioned and changes occurred. They pointed out the differences between toads and frogs and drew the visitor's attention to peculiarities of their movement. Observations by pupils had been recorded in writing and drawing, which were displayed on the walls.

Another group of pupils was busy with a small pool in which they were trying to construct an earth dam similar to those in the area that prevented flooding by creating a series of lakes. On the wall was a chart showing the results of a survey of bridges in the area, each classified according to type and the kind of material used in construction. There were paintings and sketches of different kinds of bridges, some of them drawn to scale. Four children were constructing a bridge, using straws, with some difficulty. Their teacher joined them to discuss strong and weak shapes.

In the book corner five youngsters were comfortably reading books titled *Berries Goodman*, *Little House on the Prairie*, *The Wizard of Earth Sea*, *Dorp Dead*, and *Freaky Friday*.

5

One girl was working on a large sheet of newsprint, carefully divided into sections, each one of which represented a page in a book she was writing. It was an Indian legend about how a chief called Thunderstorm got his name. In the same area, another girl was carefully finishing a crayon resist cover for a book of very fine poems she had written, while two boys were carving an Indian totem pole and discussing the meaning of the symbols they were using.

It was an interesting place, full of purposeful activity. Real investigations were taking place and being developed and recorded over a period of time; ideas were being shared and validated. It was evident that firsthand experience was valued and that materials were available for following up and testing out ideas. The climate was easy and relaxed, but students still worked productively. Here was not only an example of good education, but a slice of good living.

How could this teacher, how can any teacher, have such a classroom? It cannot be transplanted complete, as a hardy shrub, and expected to survive; it has to be sown as a seedling and allowed to grow and develop in its own soil. Such education cannot be reproduced, packaged, and delivered in "teacher proof" formats to anyone wanting something new. In a sense, the idea has to be rediscovered and created anew every time it is embraced by a new teacher or started in a new place.

INFORMAL EDUCATION DEFINED

The kind of education discussed here is a dynamic enterprise that is highly personal, continuously evolving, and forever in a state of becoming. It exists entirely for the special intellectual and social needs of the children it serves, and its development is dependent primarily on the work of the teacher as she brings children and learning opportunities together. Although informal education cannot be easily duplicated, it can be analyzed and described. It can be understood by open-minded teachers who will try to do so. The formulations underpinning it have been made explicit by such educators as Lillian Weber, Susan Isaacs, Molly Brearly, and John Dewey, and may be summarized as follows:

1. The goals are humanistic inasmuch as the total development of the child is central.
2. The child is conceived as an active agent in his own learning, bringing his individuality and learning style to the task.
3. The curriculum is planned and the classroom provisioned with the child's needs and potential for learning in mind.
4. Learning comes about as children find their own questions in real, firsthand experience and have the opportunity to pursue their investigations in the school setting.
5. Materials, conditions, and resources are such that the school facilitates and supports the learning child in his inquiry and allows him to test out and validate his findings among his peers.
6. The classroom environment reflects the teacher's degree of awareness of herself as a facilitator of learning and reveals her understanding of and confidence in the child as a learning organism.

7. The teacher's insight into the potentialities for learning in ordinary materials and her ability to see how basic concepts can be acquired through the exploration and use of materials are reflected in the provisioning and organization of the classroom.

These are the distinctive features of the kind of education discussed here—the main characteristics that distinguish "true informal education" from classrooms that only bear the label or a similar one. Sadly, informal education has become an umbrella term for a range of untraditional practices, some of which are hardly education! A half-baked notion is abroad that if you remove some of the furniture from your classroom, throw a rug in a corner, and store most of the textbooks in the supply room, you have transformed education and set children free to do their own thing, unhampered by any guidance or teaching.

These settings may be labeled "open classrooms," "informal education," or "free schools," but regrettably, some of them only contaminate a powerful idea because they do not provide good education, formal or informal. The contamination spreads and inhibits the healthy growth of good alternative classrooms when many educators, as well as casual observers, use the terms interchangeably and indiscriminatingly. Thus, the label becomes a libel, just as Edgar Dale has warned.

Many elements often equated with informal education include open-space or wall-less classrooms, carpet, multi-age grouping, or special arrangements of the furniture. These things may well enhance the learning situation, but they are only subsidiary to the central matters. When a teacher says, "The fire marshall made me get rid of my carpet and move my furniture away from the door, so I can't 'teach informal anymore,'" one wonders how she understood "informal" in the first place. She has not assimilated the central ideas at all. The very best informal classrooms I have known had four walls, no carpet, and bare floors that at times were incredibly cold. Some things thought to be essential accouterments of informal classrooms are in fact incidental; carpet and walled or open spaces fall in this category.

It is essential to know what you are about—fundamentally—as you begin to change from the traditional classroom with its well-established curriculum to a more flexible and varied situation.

8

You need to know what is important—and what is not; what is subsidiary—and what is irrelevant; what is dissonant but possibly stimulating—and what is detracting and possibly eroding.

We have identified the central focus: the child, the teacher, firsthand experience, and concrete learning materials. We have stressed the concept of the child as an active learner and the teacher as a facilitator, able to tune into her student's inquiry in a way that enables her to make resources he needs available. Her ability to do this comes from 1) real knowledge of the child, 2) her understanding of the relevant content in terms of basic concepts and conceptual relationships, and 3) her ability to see possibilities in materials and events.

Teachers often find it difficult to know how learning is initiated in informal education. If the child is to be encouraged to follow his own interests and pace his own work, then is she responsible for stimulating and directing learning? The answer is that she has a very real responsibility, but she exercises it in a different way. She has to judge when and how to intervene when a child is pursuing his personal and perhaps divergent interests. She has to know when to challenge a child with new ideas and further investigation; she has to know how to sustain him through particular difficulties, when to let something go because it is beyond his depth. She has to know how to put further resources in his way, to help him formulate new questions.

Many forward looking teachers see this new exciting way of teaching as a sort of promised land, and the urge to try it, to "get on with it," is great. Intellectually, they easily become enthusiastic about the goals and concepts that support the new practices. Many have had disquieting feelings that all was not well in their classrooms as they were going through the motions of doling out information and teaching skills. Many have felt burdened by the constant need to motivate children to *do*—to study, to read, to obey, to conform. Many others have become weary of the responsibility for covering a prescribed amount of subject matter and exhausted from continued efforts to overcome group inertia and to stimulate children to learn. Teachers want schools to be sensitive to human needs and provide opportunities for real learning. They want them to be warm, lively, humane places. But how can they become so? What is required?

9

Requirements for Informal Education

A first essential step is to shake off the "mindlessness," to use Charles Silberman's term, that shrouds current practices. The routines of time schedules, grade level groupings, report cards, letter grades, uniform testing, adopted texts, yearly promotions—the list could go on and on—need to be scrutinized in light of the serious purposes of schooling. What has happened is that these practices, which were once the facilitators of educational goals, have become more important than the intellectual development and personal fulfillment that should be the realities of education—the serious purposes.

When problems are discussed, time and time again, it is grades, test results, textbook adoptions, and pupil groupings that take precedence over trying to understand the educational process in terms of the individual child. Even in the education of the administrators, the leaders of schools, the realities are considered management matters and the ability to manipulate and maintain the system. Thus, principals become engrossed in studying politics, finance, personnel, and public relations rather than engaged in exploring learning theory, or children's intellectual and emotional development, which must be at the heart of the educational enterprise. So we thoughtlessly continue with the old habits left over from another time, when different educational purposes and values prevailed. When we begin to scrutinize the beliefs on which we act, our operational beliefs, we may be shocked to find that they differ considerably from our espoused beliefs, those that represent what we think education ought to be.

Examine Underlying Assumptions

What are the real assumptions that can be inferred from the routines cited above? Pervading much of what happens in school is the belief that there exists a core of knowledge, of subject matter, that is critical for all to possess. Aside from the need in modern society to be thoughtfully literate, one would find it extremely difficult to get universal agreement on just what that knowledge is. Yet the mastery of certain selected subject matter and skills is the basis for the routines of promotions, grades, basic textbooks, homogeneous groupings, and so on.

Closely related is the assumption that pupils learn what the teachers and textbooks teach. Such beliefs cause teachers to decide what pupils should learn, how—by which means—they should learn, when they should learn, and what should happen to those who do not learn. This has made the teacher a selector and organizer of knowledge, a teller-informer, a prescriber and director of learning, and an evaluator and judge. It has caused many teachers to concentrate on subject matter—material things—rather than on the dynamics of child learning and personality— human things. Yet almost any teacher who has given a follow-up test over what was "taught" in mathematics, grammar, or history knows that not all pupils learn what is taught. As any thoughtful teacher knows, students have an unusual capacity to revise, reconstitute, or ignore what she teaches.

Especially inhibiting are assumptions about what constitutes structure in the curriculum. Many educators behave as though the structure found in textbooks and guides is an appropriate one for young learners. They feel a certain security in having well-developed curriculum guides and adopted textbooks lined up on the shelves. They feel confident that the educational edifice will endure as long as the structure is clearly evident in texts and guides that set forth content and skills in orderly ways that alas! often conform only to adult logic.

But this belief in texts rests on a shaky assumption—that children learn subject matter and skills in the same way adults conceive them to be organized. Reading, especially, is fraught with misconceptions about what needs to be known and the sequence of getting to know it. Guides, workbooks, and checklists put forth hierarchies of skills to be mastered along the road to reading: names of letters, consonant sounds, vowel sounds, and blends. Yet the evidence suggests that children learn to read in a variety of ways and use highly personalized ways of understanding written language. Often they learn by recognizing everyday words around them—salt, pizza, hamburger, Tide, Oldsmobile. They may copy these words and begin to try out their own ideas. Knowledge of written language is assimilated as they need and use it from signs and labels, TV, and stories read to them. The fact that published reading materials are based on widely different ideas, each offered as "the complete one," makes one suspect flaws in an educational structure fabricated from a few basic texts. In responding to a question about structure while at Cornell in 1964, Piaget said:

> The question comes up whether to teach the structure, or to present the child with situations where he is active and creates structures himself—the goal in education is not to increase the amount of knowledge, but to create the possibilities for a child to invent and discover. When we teach too fast, we keep the child from inventing and discovering himself. . . . Teaching means creating situations where structures can be discovered; it does not mean transmitting structures which may be assimilated at nothing other than the verbal level. (Duckworth in Ripple and Rockcastle, 1964.)

The demoralizing aspect of predetermining structures and imposing them on children in carefully sequenced lessons is that independence in learning is thwarted, and students never know the excitement of learning by seeking, selecting, and structuring their own network of experience.

Other assumptions must be confronted, too, when the need for change arises:

1. Is learning really confined by a need to prepare children in one class for next year's class?
2. Are we to sacrifice a year of children's living and growing and learning to some kind of arbitrary demand from a future curriculum or a particular teacher's demands?
3. Do educators and parents really believe that twelve to fourteen years of narrow, barren, predetermined, prestructured educational experience paves the way for a rich, full, antonomous adult life?
4. Can the outcomes of learning in school be measured against preset performance objectives?
5. Does learning proceed best in quiet, orderly, routinized classrooms?

These are the ghosts that lurk in the curriculum corridors and rattle the chains of fear and skepticism and help to keep the old routines in vogue. They discourage all but the strong-in-heart from venturing from the well-worn paths of tradition. But laying bare the old assumptions is not sufficient to bring about change; doing so may result only in disillusion and despair. It is not sufficient to discard timeworn practices without an awareness of what to provide in their place. To become an informal teacher one must begin to understand the basic ideas that support this "new" kind of education.

Understanding Children

Visitors to good informal classrooms marvel at the quality of work underway, the involvement of children, the excellence in much of the writing, the many concrete learning materials in use, and the generally relaxed, but purposeful atmosphere. How does this happen? What keeps such learning environments alive and well?

Study of informal education reveals a cohesive philosophy of education that embraces new ways of thinking about how children learn and the role of the school in advancing their learning. It is assumed that children enter school already established as learners and well on their way in learning to learn. The task for the school is to carry on this learning, not to cut across the child's understandings and confuse his purposes with a new set of preplanned experiences.

The teacher of an informal classroom, then, must become a student of children's growth and learning. She must learn to observe children, talk with them on a one-to-one basis, and get to know them really well.

A teacher should begin by trying to *know* two or three children extremely well. She must learn to tune in precisely when a particular child begins inquiring. She does this by intelligent observation. For example, while watching children working at the water table, she talks with them and asks herself specific questions.

Is David concerned with the properties of water, the way it behaves as he pours from one container to another? What is he thinking as he pours it through a funnel connected to plastic tubing? Why is he raising and lowering the funnel? Is he concerned with the pattern it makes as it snakes along the tube? Is he concerned with whether the speed of the flow changes? Is he surprised that bending the tube alters the flow? Is he surprised that the funnel is overflowing? Does the fact that he has altered his rate of pouring indicate that he is beginning to understand and control the situation?

This kind of observation helps her see the way David plays and experiments, the kinds of organization he, himself, brings to the situation. It gives her a basis for intervention, if it is appropriate to intervene, and how to go about it. When she has established *his* purpose, then her questions and comments can be relative to it. She can help bring to his consciousness the cause and effect and give him the opportunity to organize and express in his own language the ideas forming in his mind.

The teacher may move to the sand tray and watch Mary, almost seven, finding out how many small buckets she can fill from the big red bucket full of sand. She knows that Mary is getting experience of filling and comparing containers, which eventually leads to understanding the concept of volume. When Mary completes her task and states that she filled nine small buckets, the teacher, who has observed that Mary's "filling" was anything but precise, asks if Mary thinks that John (also working in the sand) would get the same result. She helps Mary record her findings so that she can recall it. When John finds that he has filled six small buckets, a problem as to why there is this difference arises. Mary is convinced that it should be nine and sets out to prove it, and John immediately points out to her that "full" means the sand reaches the top, not just anywhere.

The teacher wants to know if John, seven and one-half years, is beginning to reverse his thinking. She asks him if he knows how many small red buckets it would take to fill the big red one. He says at once that it must be six because the full bucket had filled six small ones. She recognizes the significance of his response in relation to his development toward concrete operational thinking and notes this on his card in her record file.

These examples of the teacher at work in the informal classroom, behaving as a student of children and their learning, demonstrate two important facets of how she functions in relation to her knowledge. She sees the children working with sand and water as investigators. Her observation of them and any discussion or questioning is based on 1) her knowledge of their likely

14

developmental stage, and 2) her knowledge of the structures, or systems of learning to which their present inquiries relate—in these cases to the properties of materials and to concepts of volume and measurement.

Understanding learners, individually, is basic to informal teaching. The teacher who would become more informal and open must try to get inside her children's minds and understand their thinking. This is where she begins to change her teaching. For as she studies children, she begins to gain new insights into learning; she comes to appreciate the creative nature of children's thinking and understands the critical need for more meaningful experiences and concrete materials.

As the teacher understands how children learn, her view of teaching changes. It becomes less one of imparting knowledge and more one of diagnosing a child's stage of knowing and providing the appropriate learning situation for him.

Changing the Way One Views Subject Matter

To foster learning, rather than to impart knowledge and skills, requires teachers to revise their conceptions of subject matter. It no longer can be viewed as an end in itself, to be mastered in an orderly way, but as a resource to be sampled and used according to the needs and purposes of the learners. The range of knowledge needed by the teacher is great, but perhaps more important is her ability to conceive various areas of knowledge in terms of basic concepts and structures. If her education has been traditional, the teacher may consciously need to revise the way she considers subject matter.

One teacher trying to refocus her views of mathematics went through a period when she consciously noted shape in the environment: the oval, triangular, and circular shapes of trees; the squares, rectangles, and triangles of man-made buildings and bridges. She practiced estimating the length of corridors and stretches of pavement, often checking out her estimates in unobtrusive strides.

Over another period of time she concentrated on written language in her home-to-school environment: the road signs, street markers, names of stores, and advertisements. She tried to group the pieces of language according to the function they served—to regulate, inform, or persuade. She organized persuasive language into propaganda categories, and occasionally she collected priceless graffitti, which often provoked an interest in "found" poetry. In all of this she consciously was bringing her structural knowledge of language to bear on the everyday writing around her.

In another instance, teachers who were beginning to study informal approaches observed and analyzed the oral language used in a workshop group of fifty teachers. Their notes provided a record of when people talked and the context of the talk, and the recordings permitted an analysis of the uses of the oral language. From this examination of the talk of their peers, the teachers began to think anew about classroom talk and to practice analyzing talk as a linguist might, according to a structure based upon use. The teachers were somewhat startled by the discovery that their own talk while working in art or construction was not always focused on work but on personal things. However, when they stopped work to examine the product or problem, their talk became analytical and evaluative.

A conceptual view of knowledge frees teachers, and thus students, from the constraints of preorganized courses. It allows them to pursue knowledge in terms of their own current understandings and interests. It frees them to use subject matter to suit their personal purposes rather than to follow it slavishly.

Conceptual learning is creative and ongoing. Once a person begins to view the world in terms of the main forces, structures, or themes, one bit of learning leads to another as a network of relationships forms. A group of preservice teachers visited a restored village where Christian Indians had lived until massacred as a result of intrigue during the Revolutionary War. As they toured the village and museum they were exposed to the life and times of these Moravian Indians—homes, customs, crafts, and religious beliefs. A study of any or all of these might have emerged and would have been valuable. But the students in small groups decided to explore different concepts. The idea of subcultures intrigued one group, since the Moravians were a minority group within the Delaware Indian tribe. As the nature of conflict between these two Indian cultures was explored, the students

16

were able to compare it to problems of minority groups in twentieth century America.

Another small group explored Moravian rituals of death and dying. They traced the customs from pre-Moravian times through the Moravian culture, noting changes related to religious beliefs, and followed up by comparing those ancient practices to modern ones. This latter investigation brought new insights into the economic aspects of death and the problems of the aged, who often are separated from their loved ones and face dying alone. These teachers were learning to view social studies in a systematic way and to develop a frame of reference that was applicable to modern life as well as to an ancient culture. The learning and interest aroused in them is likely to continue to develop because of the relevance of the topics to their lives.

Experience and Appreciate Processes

Often, those teachers who move toward informal classrooms find that they literally have to turn their thinking upside-down in order to find new ways of dealing with subject matter, both in terms of content and process. Many find it difficult to appreciate the processes involved in learning because in the intervening years since their childhood they have relied increasingly on abstract verbal learning. An important part of learning to teach informally is to experience, oneself, the detailed intricate processes involved in learning many things of value, such as constructing a model bridge, representing an experience in two or three different media, or solving a real problem related to some aspect of the physical or social environment. This personal experience of learning appears to be necessary to appreciating the kinds of thinking involved, the amount of time required, and the aggravating frustrations that occur in working through a problem. Teachers have to experience anew the exhilaration of solving a problem or representing a place or an idea in a new art form.

Teachers often find that they have to rediscover what it means to work their way through a truly demanding problem. Much of the elementary teacher's time is spent helping children learn something she already knows; thus, the challenge to her own thinking is slight. By engaging a problem, however, by working it out in her own way, a teacher can appreciate the exhilaration of learning.

A young teacher of third-graders became interested in the ecological changes that would occur in a stream, Alum Creek, as a result of a dam being built to provide water and a recreation area for the surrounding metropolitan area. The dam would alter the flow of water which in turn, she learned in her investigation, would drastically influence the marine life of the creek. She became intrigued with the speed of waterflow, wondering how fast it was and what influenced the rate of flow. She hypothesized that the speed of flow was somehow related to distance from the source of the creek. Using a four-foot stick, a round detergent bottle, and several lids from cottage cheese cartons, the teacher constructed a device, somewhat like a paddle wheel, for measuring the rate of flow.

She went to several spots in the creek at regular distances from the source to measure the speed. To her consternation, she found that there was no relation at all. Her hypothesis was not working out; she could not understand why. Was it the width of the creek that made the difference? To her intense irritation, she found that this was not so either. On checking her work with her teacher, by the process of elimination, she found that one possibility she had not checked was depth. By following up this lead, she discovered that speed was related to the gradient of the bed of the creek.

She could understand, then, how the dam would greatly alter the water level and how this in turn would influence the flow and the wild life in the stream. She continued to investigate the kinds of life in the creek and learned what biologists predicted would happen to this life and the kinds of life that would probably replace it. The social-political problems became interesting too. Who made decisions about dams and such things, and on what bases were they made? How could she as a concerned citizen make her voice heard?

From examining the creek in terms of a major concept, this teacher found that she became completely engrossed in the study, and that one event led to another. Whereas her interests at first were mathematical, they later included biology and physics (the flow of water), then sociology and politics (how public decisions are made). Throughout the entire study ran the human and aesthetic concerns related to preserving the quality of life. This teacher learned about complete involvement in learning, the generative qualities of a real inquiry, the discipline demanded, and how such involvement can move one to social action. She gained a new appreciation of what it means "to learn."

Experiences of this kind are an enormous help as one changes concepts and practices in teaching. Often change involves overcoming fears of being untalented in some area, such as art or music, unskilled in constructing or caring for plants and animals, or unknowledgeable in some subject, such as oceanography. Feelings of inadequacy in the arts seem to be among the most inhibiting for teachers. Personal involvement in some form of art helps to overcome these feelings. Once teachers experience the glow of producing something that expresses their feelings or conceptions, they become more open to the next try.

A large workshop group of teachers had resisted using clay for days because, for one reason or another, they felt very little could come of it. Beyond making simple pinch pots, they were unanimous in thinking clay modeling was beyond them. Besides, it was too messy in the classroom! One morning their art instructor played some music and got the group moving, very gently at first: shuffling feet, moving hands and arms, swaying bodies; everyone moving on their feet, joining with a partner; and finally, getting into groups of five or six to portray with their bodies a group of people held together by physical force, yet exhibiting tension as some were trying to move away. The clay modeling that followed was intense. Participants approached lumps of red clay with greater confidence and sureness, having overcome much of their previous inhibition. From working through a problem physically, they were able to approach a simple problem in the clay medium with greater insight and skill. The results were unbelievable in form, line, and feeling of unity.

Changing Perceptions of Learning Materials

As soon as teachers begin seriously to link into children's experience and carry it forward, and to value process in learning

19

along with product, their concept of learning materials expands to include a wide array of concrete materials and firsthand experiences. Learning which starts with what a child knows or cares about usually begins with the here and now: a new baby in the family, a fishing trip, football scores, food, clothing, or creatures inhabiting the pond near the school.

Likewise, believing that pupils learn from doing—their doing—and from acting on concrete materials and situations, the teacher's job becomes one of presenting appropriate materials and experiences for the student to explore, try out, or reconstruct. Provisioning the classroom with an abundance of concrete materials and arranging them so that they are easily available to children is a critical step on the road to child-centered learning.

Much has been written about learning materials for informal classrooms. Experienced teachers have developed lists of basic materials that are needed in every classroom. A range of good art papers, paint, and reliable adhesives as well as various kinds of measuring instruments come in this category. But securing materials and organizing centers will not create, magically, a more exciting or intellectually challenging classroom. First, a teacher must begin to see material in terms of its possibilities for stimulating pupils to learn in *her* class. She cannot always include—lock, stock, and barrel—materials from another teacher's list. I asked a headmistress of an infant school what *basic* learning materials were used in the classes. She thoughtfully replied, "There's sand, water, paint, paper, reliable paste, blocks, and measuring devices and good books!"

In providing for young children, the teacher would likely think of such things as essential and also include other material such as animals and plants, simple musical instruments, materials for weighing and measuring, a magnifying glass, and good story books and reference books. With older children, the school site or some interesting section of local terrain may be the primary source of learning. Or children may study the music and art of an early Indian tribe or the westward movement of pioneers.

As these various interests appear, the teacher should think through possible directions they might go and obtain the needed resources. The materials she provides should help students translate ideas, pictures, and verbal information into different forms, often more concrete or aesthetic. Concern with the opening up of the West undoubtedly would bring interest in Conestoga wagons, the prairie, log cabins, sod houses, Indians, and buffalo. The need for both appropriate information sources and construction materials to create a wagon, sod house, or a prairie terrain is apparent.

Most of the materials mentioned are basic and in constant use so the teacher must keep them replenished. Other types of materials are specific to a particular content area or to different stages of work. For example, children who have shifted from using nonstandard to standard measures need a range of instruments: tape measures, yard and meter sticks for measuring length, a surveyor's tape for working in larger areas. Access to different types of weight measures—scales and weights, compression scales, a spring balance, and a simple balance—allow much greater choice and precision when working on different problems.

Teachers often ask what materials are of greatest value and which centers should be established first. For informal education materials should be provided and centers created in response to children's learning needs. If children are to go beyond ordinary textbooks and project reports in social studies, for example, the immediate need for a center supplied with tools and creative materials will become apparent. Children can take part in planning and organizing the center. When they share in decisions about material, they can better visualize possibilities and make best use of the center.

In the beginning stages, many teachers find the first area to organize is one containing art and allied creative materials. It helps to think of it as a workshop; provide easy access and storage so that children can reasonably be expected to prevent it from becoming a mess. Consideration for the cleaning staff must be kept in mind. Try to establish the creative work center near a sink and have available good cleanup materials. It is a good idea to keep the center away from the door where someone might easily knock over an easel or stumble over a box of scrap materials. However, if your only source of water is in the corridor or girls' lavatory down the hall, do have your paint, clay, and construction center along a wall adjacent to the corridor door, but not spilling over in front of it.

Do provide two or three manageable buckets for clean water and dirty water, labeled so that even the youngest child can cope. Do contrive a storage facility which will accommodate jars of paint, paint brushes, paper of varying sizes and quality, wire, string, bits of foil, staples and staple gun, thumb tacks and butterfly fasteners, rolls of wallpaper and wallpaper books, and neatly covered and labeled boxes and bins for such precious donations as velvet ribbon, sequins, beads, and copper wire.

Inadequate haphazard storage can be the downfall of otherwise promising art production. When pupils cannot find the materials or have difficulty returning unused materials, they tend to make do with what is at hand and trample over what is left. The most harmful outcome, likely, is the failure of children to develop real respect for materials.

In like manner, as the work in mathematics and science enlarges to include practical work on specific concepts, for example measurement, time, shape symmetry, or probability, the need for mathematical materials will become apparent. The pupils will recognize with their teacher the need for tape measures, yardsticks, string, canes, drinking straws, and surveyor's tapes; clocks, egg timers, candles, and a stop watch; mirrors, mosaics, balls of different sizes, wheels, tins, lids, geometric board, and rubber bands; paper for folding and cutting, squared paper, colored pens and pencils. They will recognize, also, the need for proper care and storage of materials and for work space.

The various materials in the art and mathematics centers are especially valuable because they can be used not only to extend or enrich learning in content areas but are also valuable sources of expression in themselves. The child messing about with paper and paint, mosaics, and geometric shapes often becomes interested in making designs or experimenting with constructions. Materials may serve as the starting point for significant learning. For example, Tim became interested in the reflectivity of various materials and found ways of testing and organizing them according to types of material and their reflective property.

Reorganizing the Classroom

The informal classroom is a workshop containing materials centers, working bays, and comfortable quiet areas for relaxation and reading. A desk and chair for each child is usually not necessary, since children move around from one work area to another. Verbal descriptions and motion pictures of informal classrooms show them as alive, warm, desirable places to be. Thus, many decide to begin by removing some of the furniture and organizing the rest into learning/materials centers and work areas. While this approach works for some teachers with some children, it can be disastrous for others. To change the room organization before the teacher and pupils have actually experienced a curriculum change often merely changes the outward form of education while leaving the old beliefs and practices intact.

One young teacher, as a result of a summer workshop in informal education, completely reorganized her second-grade classroom. She stored about one-third of the chairs; pushed individual desks together to make long tables for work; set up mathematics, art, and reading centers; and secured materials for cooking in the classroom. But the children were not accustomed to working alone, except in workbooks or worksheets; they expected to have their own desk and chair and did not know how to work with concrete mathematics materials without considerable teacher supervision. They were worried about what to tell their parents about reading since they were not meeting daily in their traditional reading groups.

The teacher was confronting problems that she had not anticipated: how to provide for each child without worksheets and workbooks; how to get children to cooperate, take turns, and care for materials; how to get children to follow through and complete tasks; and how to satisfy herself and the principal that the children were really learning and making progress in what she considered the essentials of primary education.

The teacher found that she was still engaged in an internal conflict about what constituted good education for young children. She worried about the effects of giving up the daily reading group. While she observed that children enjoyed cooking, she was uncertain about its contribution to learning.

Her uncertainty inevitably communicated itself to the children. Their disregard for classroom activities increased and showed itself in apathetic and disruptive behavior. Needless to say, the experiment in informal education was soon abandoned; the teacher overcame her feelings of guilt and disappointment by turning to "more reliable" methods: three reading groups plus independent work using ditto sheets, workbook pages, an art activity for those who do their work quickly, and a desk and chair for everyone!

A more gradual move will likely be more enduring and satisfying for both pupils and teachers. Transform the room only when curriculum changes permit a different working space and a greater use of concrete materials, when children become more involved in active learning.

Change in the upper grades might come about through the extension of children's interests in almost any problem or topic, such as any of those mentioned earlier. Or a group might choose to explore shapes, scientifically or aesthetically, as they are used in structures in the environment. Sketches and photographs can be made, perhaps also three dimensional models. They will raise questions why some shapes are more frequently used in certain structures than others. The need to experiment with shapes in various kinds of structures, to verify hunches about which have the greatest strength under various conditions may well arise. The need to build, test, record, and display work generates the need to reorganize the classroom—to regroup furniture, substitute a long table for some student desks, create more display space, devise functional units for storing materials, and to set up work areas that permit a safe flow of traffic and preserve a quiet area.

There is perceptible logic in the organization of a well-functioning informal classroom. If older pupils help to establish and maintain it in response to learning needs, it will probably function reasonably well. Teachers of young children have more responsibility for setting up the class themselves, but they should involve the children whenever possible.

The following guidelines may be useful to teachers wanting to change the physical aspects of their classrooms:

1. The classroom is a workshop for learning; it is arranged with the requirements of that learning in mind.

2. Consideration is given to who will work in the classroom—their physical size, their ability to manage tools and materials of different sizes and shapes, their general modes of learning, their potential interests, and their basic physical and intellectual

needs. It is useful to have some papers and materials precut. Materials should be stored at or below the children's eye-level, and work space should be at a level comfortable for them.

3. The kind of learning that will likely occur is forecast, and the basic materials needed and space required are identified. Teachers of five- to seven-year-olds should reserve a space for dramatic play and for construction and work with large blocks. Sand and water will be used to teach mathematical concepts of weight and volume and sorting natural and man-made materials will teach classification.

Teachers of middle-grade youngsters might well consult the basic mathematics textbook to ascertain what concepts are presented so that they can forecast the concrete materials that children are likely to require to learn concepts through their own action. Appropriate storage must be found, too, if materials are to be used and yet cared for so that they will be readily available for all. Long canes, doweling, and metric and yardsticks are often found to be most troublesome to store. Sturdy round or square cardboard boxes at least two-thirds the height of the tallest rods serve nicely—and attractively—when painted or covered with contact paper or plastic coated wallpaper.

4. It helps to consider multiple uses of some materials. This perhaps will influence the quantity needed as well as where they are stored. String, ribbon, and rope are as likely to be needed in sewing and art projects as in mathematics. Many teachers find making a simple diagram of potential uses of selected materials valuable (See Figure 1).

Such charts help to make decisions about organizing materials that have general use. It is a mistake to restrict children to using materials in specific areas. The centers are really ways of organizing materials and tools so that each child knows where things are kept. The simpler the organization is, the more likely it will work.

5. Consider the nature of various activities. Some work involves more talk and noise than others. Woodworking construction and block building and other noisy activities should be placed as far away as possible from quiet areas reserved for discussions, reading, and writing. Art and cooking activities require water; therefore, they should be near the supply. If water must

come from outside, then the art work area probably should be along the wall adjacent to, but clear of, the door.

6. Providing for good visibility in a classroom where working bays are often partially screened off by bookshelves, storage units, or display boards requires some ingenuity. However, if the teacher is to fulfill her role as a diagnostic observer, guide, and resource to children, she must be able to observe what is underway by a quick look around the room, even though she is engaged with children in one area.

When a primary grade teacher secludes herself with two or three children on the floor behind tall bookcases and screens for twenty minutes or so, she is asking for trouble. She will miss critical observations of learning, not to mention the accidents or behavior incidents that might have been avoided.

7. Keep ease of movement, general flow of traffic, and safety in mind when reorganizing the classroom. Unnecessary accidents and conflict are avoided when everyone can move about without bumping into each other and knocking things over. The teacher can help her students more readily if she can get to them. Try to make certain that storage units are sturdy and will not topple over.

8. Try to see the room from a child's point of view. A headmistress in a London school reports that her teachers kneel in the center of their classrooms. She explains that they are not praying but trying to see the room through a child's eyes. If you sit on the floor or a student's chair you will know if the children see a cavernous place with strips of paper and cardboard drooping down off the walls or an organized working space complete with tools and materials and attractive displays of work within their line of vision.

9. Give attention to the aesthetic qualities of the classroom too. Make it inviting to children; nurture their visual senses with color and good design in various media. The way a teacher arranges displays and furniture or reproductions of art contribute to this aesthetic development. Some teachers have made a point of collecting fabrics; others have sought everyday products of good design, such as pieces of pottery, wooden bowls, or toys. Above all provide adequate space, too, for displaying children's three-dimensional products as well as their flat pieces of work.

10. As activities in the class change, so will the need to change the physical arrangement arise. The more children are brought into thinking about the use of the room and help in its reorganization the more they will be able to use it efficiently and the more they will want to care for it.

Figure 1

Material	Math Measurement	Math Volume	Math Pattern Relations	Model Building	Sewing	Art Collage
Canes, Doweling, Wood Slats	✓		✓	✓		
Yarn, Ribbon, Felt	✓			✓	✓	✓
Miniature People, Cars, Animals	✓	✓	✓		✓	

Potential Use

COPING WITH NEW TEACHING ROLES

Once teachers begin to conceive of children as capable of making choices and initiating and processing their own experiences, the whole process of education changes. Subject matter is dealt with differently, conceptions of what constitutes learning materials are revised, and the role the teacher plays is completely revolutionized. The new role worries some teachers, and a few find it uncomfortable. Once the formality of the traditional classroom is gone, teachers become uncertain about their relationships with pupils, about discipline matters, and particularly about directing learning or even giving information. With the old forms and rituals out of the way, the teacher's role is more nebulous and will remain so until new conventions are established.

Occasionally a teacher who is beginning to embrace the concepts of informal education misinterprets the appropriate work of the teacher and concludes that as children become more active in learning, she should become more passive. Thus, she avoids directing the children or refrains from expecting them to work at a reasonable standard or to pursue an investigation in some depth.

The teacher's responsibility, however, is to further children's learning. That is the unique function of the school. To achieve this, the teacher in an informal classroom has special responsibilities.

Creates Conditions

She makes available the appropriate conditions for learning. She determines, secures, organizes materials and experiences which children will find interesting and challenging, as described earlier in this booklet. She tries to provide for variety, continuity, and balance in the curriculum. She is responsible for not only providing the physical environment but for designing a rigorous learning curriculum that is based on understanding how children learn and knowledge of subject matter and materials.

Relates to Children

She relates to children and guides their learning, as individuals and as members of groups. Questions often arise in regard to teacher-pupil relationships. How friendly should I get with my pupils? Should they address me by my first name? How far do I go in disciplining them? Is there ever any group work or is it all individual?

Many of these problems vanish as the focus centers more and more on the ongoing learning in which the teacher participates as co-learner, as the person she is, as well as a teacher. The more she can become an interested co-learner, truly delighted along with the child when he discovers he can mix and control a new color, for example, the less she will think about herself. Uncertainties about teacher-pupil relations, group-individual instruction, and teacher directed learning become clearer once pupils and teacher are truly engaged with learning. The teacher will find herself relating in a friendly way to each child. It will be similar to discussing with an adult friend the color scheme for decorating a bedroom, for example. In that relationship, neither adult is consciously teaching the other, even if one is more expert at interior decoration. Rather, they explore all the possibilities together, sharing and criticizing, discarding and finding new possibilities. The child will appreciate being able to talk in this way, knowing he can rely upon the teacher's interest and support.

The teacher enters into a mutual learning relationship with children, but she does not have to become a peer. She is there to provide help beyond that of the peer group. Whether pupils use the teacher's Christian name or surname is unimportant except as it relates to school practice, community custom, and what is comfortable for both teachers and pupils. Familiar address will not in itself result in better relationships between teacher and child; nor will formal titles inhibit them. The quality of communication and concern between the two makes for enduring ties. Engaging in conversation with children on a one-to-one basis or in small groups helps to establish this bond, especially if the teacher listens and allows the conversation to follow the children's interests.

When school work is concerned with investigating things of mutual interest to pupils, groups will form naturally. At other times individuals will work alone depending on the task. Two children often work together because many tasks require two pairs of hands. Estimating the length of the corridor in yards or strides, for example, is more easily done and recorded if two children participate. Although much of the reading and writing are pursued on an individual basis, a great deal can be gained by organizing small groups to discuss some commonly read books or to share their work under the guidance of the teacher.

Challenges Children to Learn

Teachers need not be timid about suggesting activities to pupils nor to encourage them to do better or more work. A teacher of nine- to eleven-year-olds had three or four apathetic youngsters who seemed quite content to just sit or to sit and read. As they were not bothering anyone, he could have left them in their state of semiconsciousness. However, he believed that something should happen to children in school that complements what happens at home; namely, guided learning. He set two boys to making butterfly nets from the net bags in which vegetables are packaged. They took their nets into the school grounds to see what they could capture. When they returned to class, they were excited and delighted with their trophies of two butterflies and a firefly!

The teacher produced a magnifying glass to encourage careful examination and description of the butterflies. Soon other children gathered round to look, too; there was excitement and interest. There were two different kinds of butterflies. In what way were they different? And comments: "I just never noticed butterflies before." There are a host of marvelous phenomena about which children may never notice if teachers do not call attention to them.

Asks Critical Questions

Sometimes insightful questions are needed to focus a child's attention on a detailed or critical aspect of a new experience. Laurie, age nine, captured a firefly in her homemade net and followed the teacher's suggestion that she might paint it, using it as a model. The firefly was enclosed in a "blister," examined under the microscope, and Laurie began to paint. It soon became apparent that she did not know how to look, how to observe closely.

The teacher asked very specific questions to help Laurie observe. "How are the wings folded?" he asked. "Are they folded on the back of the insect or alongside the body? Are they soft gauze-like wings, or hard-cased ones? How is the head joined to the body? What about the eyes?" He was not sure of the child's previous experience of fireflies. She called them lightning bugs, and he told her the other name and asked if she knew why the insect had been given names like these. It was obvious she was not aware of their peculiar quality, and he considered how to help her make the connection. Meantime she continued her painting with some new understanding.

In this example, the teacher's questions grew out of his intention to further the child's knowing about fireflies. He first tried to find out what the child was centering on—first from observation and then by asking specific questions. He tried further to link the child's past experience to the present. He focused on an important aspect of the learning experience and helped the child begin to acquire some observational skills. The teacher's ability to ask questions resulted more from his observation of the learner and his knowledge of fireflies—the content—than from his expertise in questioning.

The ability to ask appropriate questions appears to be essential in guiding pupils' learning, and various short courses and instructional strategies are available to help teachers develop these skills. Many are excellent and foster an understanding of categories of questions, purposes for questioning, and the relationship between questioning and thought. However, more than an understanding of systems of questioning is needed, for they can easily become a hollow practice and a means of harrassing the learners.

Teachers will find themselves able to ask more insightful questions if they concentrate on 1) knowing children better so that they detect their immediate interests and 2) maintaining their personal zest for learning, including efforts to grasp a conceptual understanding of various fields of knowledge. Through knowing pupils personally and enjoying learning experiences, teachers will become aware of what is important to bring to children's attention and find a way to bring this about through discussion and raising questions.

There is research evidence that shows teachers tend to talk too much and ask too many unimportant questions. (A mindless verbal ping-pong.) The skillful informal teacher listens more; she links her questions to a child's experience and carries it on in relation to the critical concepts in a field.

Coping with Behavior Problems

A terrifying question teachers ask as they consider changing from traditional ways of working is, "How can I be sure 'a little bit of chaos' won't become a lot?" Many who have written about informal education have implied a fine line between freedom and chaos, suggesting that when individuals are actively—physically—involved in work, some chaos is likely or inevitable. If fears of complete disorder are warranted, then one only can be alarmed at the anarchy smoldering beneath the authoritarian rule of traditional classrooms.

The theme of this fastback is that change in living and learning in the classroom should be rational. It implies multifaceted changes, all arising from reason and purpose. From the beginning the advice has been to rethink and plan parts of the environment in response to needs arising from new ways of learning. It is assumed that children will be aware of the purposes, the plans, and the possible outcomes of these activities; they will see the reasons. If so, a big part of the behavior battle is won. It is when children sit or wander about aimlessly that incidents occur that may well flare into major disturbances. The teacher helps children develop self-control and independence by getting them involved in an engrossing learning situation. This is fundamental; it is at the heart of developing autonomous, socially sensitive children.

If children are bored and aimless, the risk of disruptive, inconsiderate behavior is high. When they are involved and interested, most behavior problems cease to exist. The following example comes from a class of inner-city fourth- and fifth-graders, not many of whom would be regarded as particularly academic. In many schools they might well be listless and apathetic or very difficult and uncooperative. In the following example the teacher and student teacher arranged a field trip into the country where children could observe birds and wild flowers, study life in a creek, and wonder at the decay of crumbling lichen-covered logs. The class became involved in preparing for the trip, arranging transportation, and contacting parent escorts.

The teacher and her student teacher planned to have some children engage in map making, ranging from simple pictorial representation to scale plans. These skills were tried out, first in the school by making a floor plan of parts of the school (since the whole was too complicated), a map of the school grounds, and maps of "How I get to school." The need for measuring devices became apparent to the children, and the teachers were ready with strips of tape, reels of binding tape for longer measures, and lengths of plain wood battening that could be cut and marked into yards and meters. This project itself involved an understanding of mathematical relations and an appreciation of using the appropriate tool for measuring.

There was discussion about the kinds of creatures they might seek, ways of observing birds, common and less common plants to look for. They made decisions and compiled lists of types of containers they would need for carrying things back to school: sketching and rubbing materials as well as instruments for observing such as magnifying glasses and binoculars, not to mention the carefully made measuring devices.

Everyone was caught up in purposeful and harmonious activity. The teachers were greatly pleased to note that the hum of work could by no means be confused with chaos and discord. Materials were put away, finished work was carefully put where it could be seen, and genuine interest in the work of peers was evident. This was an authentic situation: the plans were real, the materials would be used, and one day's work led into the next. The plans and talk centered about seeing something and doing something, rather than on doing some mathematics, doing some reading, doing some spelling, writing, and so on. For a week, at least, the classroom was concerned with learning in much the same way that real people outside school learn.

Teachers need to know their pupils well so that they can anticipate problems and make reliable inferences about their likely needs and interests. Thus they can anticipate and ward off disrupting events and can sense when they should intervene.

Having some understanding of the cultural customs of the children helps to interpret behavior; for example, the Indian or Mexican child who does not answer when the teacher speaks but looks at the floor or the preadolescent black boys who shout at each other, calling names, and pushing and jostling each other about. Her knowledgeable observation of the latter incident may lead to the conclusion that the boys are merely "playing" a speech event (shucking), quite natural among black teens and preteens and not embroiled in a serious struggle. In the first instance, she will be aware that the silence and averted eyes may be a cultural heritage rather than defiance or disrespect.

The teacher has to know when to intervene and when to ignore or overlook. Seven-year-old David entered the classroom one hot summer morning engaged in a verbal battle with Nancy, about a year older. The teacher noted that even as the shouts grew more intense, David began to work building a boat. She did not try to restrain him but got Nancy involved in a project. She was testing her hunch that David would cease his screaming when he discovered it was not getting results.

Informal classrooms are free of many of the restrictive rules long associated with schools: talking in class, cooperating on work, lining up, being taken to the lavatory or marched to the art room. However, greater freedom in class and wide use of the school building and grounds create a need for practical limits, for some ground rules. These should be absolutely clear to children but not handed out as an absolute code. In general they should grow out of practical situations. Even five- and six-year-olds can see that too many people spoil the block play. So a rule emerges: Only four people can play with blocks. If tools are left wherever last used, they are not available for others; thus, a rule is formed.

Always concerned about safety, the teacher is alert to the way children use tools. If Bobby is about to jab someone with a screwdriver, she takes it from him immediately, saying, "You'll hurt Mary! Screwdrivers are not for hurting people but for tightening screws. Let me know when you want to use it properly." Bobby is not personally berated by the teacher, but told concisely what the rules are and *why*.

Caring for tools and equipment and cleaning up need not be quite the problem it often is. Having well-marked accessible places for tools, reminding children to return things, helping children clean up as they finish using tools and materials instead of waiting until the end of the day all help to get good habits established. If the teacher joins children in cleaning up, the work is not so hard, and she shows in action how to complete certain tasks efficiently.

A tray of sewing materials was knocked down by a couple of six-year-olds. Thread, yarn, elastic, and dozens of buttons were scattered all over the floor. The teacher did not make this an issue of goodness and badness. The rule was simply that if you make a mess you clear it up. In this case, the teacher said, "Come on, I'll help you. We'll sort them out and put them in their right places." In fact, a learning experience of classification emerged from what began as an accident.

EVALUATION OF LEARNING

As the learning goals and activities of education change, evaluation practices must change, too. Old techniques will not suit new, expanded kinds of learning. Values change, and the essence of e-*valu*-ation is being concerned about what is truly of value in a venture. The teacher reveals what she values about a piece of work and about people everytime she confers with a child or responds to something he has produced. Here we have a piece of writing from Pippa, who is just eight:

the Wood

the Sqivells are scampering
and running about, ~~Now~~ *Now* and
then they stop and gather
a nut then off they
run Scampering up a tree.

trunk careing a nut in there
moth. the deer are restin
under the oak and the
Berds are singing there
best songs and in the
midst of hesel and Basel
the cookoo cokoo's one long
and loud cooocoo.

then All intheforist are still, for
the coocoo has siad the hanters
are comeing then all of a saden
there is a great rush it lasts
unt.ll All are seaf in there
Wood. then in comes the
henter's on horses of Beaty
~~Bert~~ the henters soon spot

a gay yong deer. thoe
they Gallop there fastest
they can not Kach up
with the gay yong
Deer frisking far in front
soon the henter's are
teird out and home they
go aguin. and the foristes
hustel and Bastel Begens
aguin untill the coco
cokoos agiun.

the
End

PiPPa

38

How does the teacher respond to this writing? What does she say to the child? Does she comment on the smudges on the paper, mark the misspelled words, or ask the child to make a neat copy? Does she dismiss it with a comment, "It's a wonderful story," and put a happy face on it? Does she notice the language used, for example, to describe the squirrel scampering in the trees and the way she has created the setting for the action of the hunter, the gay young deer, and the cuckoo giving the warning?

Previously, it has been suggested that the teacher become a co-learner with her students. In this instance the teacher might become a co-author, tuning into the child's work and commenting on how the story builds up, on the suspense of the chase, and on the choice of words used to describe the animals and action. She is emphasizing valued aspects of writing: the content, style, and general feeling communicated. These are the important things to foster, for without them, what is there?

At this stage she will be very selective in her comments to the child about mechanics and spelling. The story shows clearly that the writer is well on the way to understanding spelling and handwriting; she has a good sense of sound-symbol relationships, and writing is legible. Depending upon previous experiences, the teacher may want to call attention to a word or two, for example, by asking, "Do you remember anything special about "q" when we use it in words?" With this bit of focusing, the child's attention will be drawn to the fact that "q" is always followed by "u"; a bit more has been added to her understanding of writing.

This represents the kind of e-valu-ing that goes on day in and day out in good informal classrooms. The evaluation is continuous, it is definitely related to the specific goals (values) inherent in the learning; it is concerned with the growth of individuals; the process is personal and timely; the focus is on qualities that are important in an area of work; and those things that are subsidiary to the work—spelling and handwriting in the above instance—remain in a subsidiary role. This kind of evaluation encourages children to write and grow. They will sense what is important in writing from the teacher's comments and also from the responses of classmates with whom the story is shared.

Many teachers are convinced that children's growth can be most clearly demonstrated if a folder is kept for each child into which representative pieces of their work are placed regularly. This folder would contain written work relating to math, social studies, or literature; that is, writing with some purpose, not just creative writing assignments. It would also contain work to do with mathematics or pieces of art; in fact, a collection covering a range of ongoing interests. Over a period of time teachers should be able to see clearly the kind of progress individual children are making. They would have something to share with parents at conferences, from which parents would likely get infinitely more information than they ever could from report cards.

Record Keeping

Many teachers use file cards, one for each child, as a quick and reliable way of keeping a record of the major events in a child's day. She jots down immediately books read, mathematical understandings, scientific explorations, and so on. Older children can be asked to enter some of the information themselves. The quickly written note will help the teacher recall the event. For example, "Made own printing devices from potato—exciting pattern," will recall the child's exploration. The cards give a quick picture of the range of work the child has been involved in. They let the teacher know, too, if she is missing out on any child, not making sufficient contact with him during the day.

Important notes or a composite evaluation can be quickly transferred to the teacher's record book where reading, math, or writing may be kept as separate subjects. There will also be a place for information that is specially valued in good education. The concern is towards general growth, attitudes toward people and to school in general; not only whether the child can read, but if he *does* read. How does he respond to literature? To music and art? Does he show growing independence and self-direction? These are the values inherent in informal education, and they must become a significant part of evaluation.

Any information having to do with periodic assessment of growth must be recorded. A variety of procedures, in addition to those given above, may be used to secure new kinds of data that are more reliable than that provided by many standardized tests now widely used. Selected Piagetian tests (e.g., for conservation or inclusion) will give insight into reasoning abilities; the informal reading inventory will provide information about reading level and comprehension, a reading miscue analysis will give clues to the language and thought processes the child uses in reading, and syntactic measures, such as the Hunt T-unit, will reveal growth in both oral and written syntax. Evaluation tools must be compatible with the goals of informal education.

Goals and Planning

In informal education teachers make special effort to link evaluation to goals and planning, to learning procedures, and to record keeping, all of which are interrelated. Everyday planning arises from an assessment of the events and outcome of the day. These events are recorded and form a basis for planning the next day. For example, a teacher may have a note on a record card for Peter that says, "worked with simple fractions—doesn't really understand equivalence." This is her assessment of Peter's engagement with math. In her plans she will specifically provide for Peter's further work on this concept.

Good planning needs to have two aspects, long-term and short-term. Long-term planning is concerned with major areas of the curriculum, the concepts being focused on during a term, or even a year, such as *Growth and Change*. She will select specific aspects of the concepts that relate to the children in her class, children whose interests, strengths and weaknesses, and past experience she will know. She brainstorms the selected areas and begins to plan very specifically.

Consider, for example, long-term planning of mathematics. A close examination of the textbook for concepts underlying the workbooks and examples will give the teacher an idea of where to start. If youngsters are to be involved with area, for example, she can think through the way this concept develops from the first covering of space to really understanding and using the concept. She may well find her children's understanding spread along the continuum.

This thinking through and around likely concepts as a way of planning is invaluable. It alleviates the day-to-day worrying about what the children will do tomorrow. Their interests and choices will be included if the initial planning is related to their known needs and interests and if the teacher provides guidance rather than prescription.

It is essential to be clear-minded in planning for informal education. This is what makes the difference between the bland, "Let's all be happy" atmosphere and the serious education that involves, that challenges, that satisfies. Anyone who thinks that becoming an informal teacher means giving up lesson plans can think again! It is the way of planning, not the fact of planning, that changes.

BEYOND THE CLASSROOM

Throughout this booklet the teacher and the classroom entity have been the focal point, and everything presented has been within this context. Many features, procedures, and people have been omitted, not because they are unimportant, but because the ever-growing teacher and the classroom environment she creates are the critical concerns. If children's learning under the teacher's guidance comes into fruition and children are working with purpose and commitment, many problems related to the school and community will be solved. When the classroom is open and functioning well, the value of the work is soon evident to all who are concerned—parents, school administrators, and colleagues. A few comments about the wider context within which the teacher works may be useful to those who are now contemplating change.

Relations with Colleagues

Bear in mind that the school is a social system within which each person works and each classroom functions. For the sake of everyone who works there, it must be an integrated environment where communication is open and the staff actively work toward common goals. Every effort must be made to establish and maintain a common expectation for pupil growth and agreement about the way the school will function.

Any teacher beginning to implement informal methods must be wary about setting herself apart as unique or better—or even different—from her colleagues. Most innovations carry a halo during the initial implementation periods. Becoming involved in

43

change is exhilarating; other energetic people are involved, too, and there may be widespread discussion and publicity. The temptation to feel a part of the elite set is great, and the inclination to state, "I'm doing it" or "I'm one of the *informal* teachers," soon becomes a habit. It sets one apart from the crowd and part of the in group.

Such attitudes, however, are contrary to the formulations of informal education, which advocates respect for all people and maintaining an educational environment where all children and teachers can flourish. Such environments are not likely to exist where a staff is torn apart either by the elitist imaginings of some people or the die-hard conservatism of others.

Relations with Parents

The informal classroom can be a startling experience for many parents; it is unlike anything from their own school experience and so may require getting used to. Most parents are well satisfied with school if their children are learning and happy. If instructional practices are gradually changed in a way the teacher can handle and if pupils are involved in making the transitions, the news going home is likely to be clear and make sense to parents. It is when pupils are suddenly put in an environment they do not understand that the message going home is bewildering. No grand announcements about innovations underway in your classroom are necessary. Be sure that any changes you make are backed by sound reasoning, but do not talk about them as earth-shaking events. Keep in mind that the aim of whatever is attempted is to improve education for your children.

Be reasonably certain about your work so that when parents ask specific quesions, for example, about reading or science projects, you can be explicit about what is underway, the reason for it, and what you expect to come from it. Since parents learn a great deal from active participation in school as resource persons, escorts on field trips, assistants in maintaining classroom equipment, class or school librarians, and many other helpful ways, make sure they know they are welcome. One parent's satisfying day with children in a real learning situation is soon communicated to others.

Relations With Administration

Ideally informal education will be initiated in a school by several teachers and the principal working together. They will be seeking similar goals for pupils and sharing the struggles and satisfaction of creating stimulating learning climates. When the principal works alongside the teachers, as is often reported about English head teachers, he is always a part of what is happening, so keeping him informed or explaining activities to him are unnecessary. However, if he is not personally involved and tends to see his role as a facilitator of teacher's innovations, then you must find ways to get him into the classroom, sharing children's work and working with them when possible so that he too can get some insight into children's learning and understand the real purposes of informal education. There is no way a principal can remain ignorant of the work in the classroom and still be a facilitator of the kind of learning underway there. When he realizes that most elementary school children need firsthand, real experiences and the materials with which to follow them up, then he will conclude that textbooks serve best when they extend and enrich learning rather than serve as the main source or, sadly, often the only source of learning. He may begin to persuade the school board that adopting and providing a textbook for each of twenty-five children in a class makes for more limited resources than buying two or three copies of a wider range of books.

He also may help them to see how restricting district-wide adoptions can be to schools that really think about education in terms of the needs and interests of the Chucks and Lindas in their own school, in their own classes. He may even persuade central administration to appropriate a greater portion of the budget on consumable materials, such as paint, art materials, sand, and construction materials, and to recognize the need to provide such things as a range of essential weighing and measuring instruments, musical instruments, and a wide range of excellent literature.

This does not imply that informal education needs to be costly and extravagant, but rather, the educational budget should be spent in ways that facilitate up-to-date, sound education and allow individual schools much more autonomy in using their allocation of available resources. This could well include money for materials children need urgently for such things as pet food, cooking materials, wire for a homemade vivarium, wood and wallboard for screens and work spaces, or even a few books chosen by the children from the local book store. There is no reason to believe that American teachers are less able to handle money allocated in this way than their British counterparts, who have long enjoyed this freedom.

A teacher interested in change should see her principal as her closest ally, even if he does not always share her views on education. She must accept that he, too, is concerned with giving children the best education they can get. This is why it is essential that he get into the classroom and be involved as children are getting on with learning. Gradually, common goals will become apparent and separate perceptions of a good learning environment will move closer.

Who Effects Change

The folly of thinking that change can be initiated by edit, from top administration *down*, or by persuasion, from outside innovators *in*, needs to be mentioned. The *idea* of informal teaching can be initiated by many different people—teachers, principals, curriculum workers, or college teachers; they can inform, demonstrate, inspire and create excitement about informal procedures. However, successful informal teaching can be achieved only as teachers change their perceptions of teaching and learning and decide to change their classroom environments. When others attempt to effect sweeping changes in schools, often it is only the outward form of the innovation that is implemented. Similarly, teachers who decide to "go informal" before they have an adequate grasp of the basic concepts and procedures involved find, also, that they are merely practicing the routines, the rituals, of the idea.

Change must come from within as needs are perceived and acted upon from personal knowledge and conviction. One wonders at the lack of understanding of the leadership within some educational systems when decisions regarding instructional change are made that endanger the personal growth and professional status of teachers. Such decisions from outside, whether they concern the type of curriculum or the teaching materials, threaten teachers' further professional growth and tend to make them dependent. As Edward Chittenden has maintained in *The Open Classroom Reader,* "schools can foster common sense and creative involvement in their teachers or they can nurture mindlessness and convention."

The theme throughout this fastback has been that informal education is centered on the creative involvement and growth of individuals. The development of individuals through their own *actions* on materials and the environment is the central purpose. Autonomy of people through experiencing success from their own actions is the desired outcome. The achievement of true autonomy for students in our schools can be attained only as their teachers experience it. Informal education is always in a state of becoming, evolving, which results from the continuous growth and change of those persons concerned with it—teachers, pupils, administrators, parents, and others.

BIBLIOGRAPHY

This bibliography extends that in the fastback by Vito Perrone, *Open Education: Promise and Problems,* and especially includes sources related to understanding child development and active learning.

Blitz, Barbara. *The Open Classroom: Making It Work.* Boston: Allyn and Bacon, 1973.

   Insightful, refreshing book giving teachers real information about beginning informal education. Many practical suggestions related to child guidance and behavior.

Bremer, Anne and John Bremer. *Open Education: A Beginning.* New York: Holt, Rinehart and Winston, 1972.

   A metaphor of change as teachers in one school increasingly asked, and responded to—, "What more can I do?"

Brearley, Molly, ed. *The Teaching of Young Children: Some Applications of Piaget's Learning Theory.* New York: Schocken Books, Inc., 1970.

   Gives the main considerations to be taken into account when planning the education of young children. Descriptions of good practice in open learning are provided within a framework of sound principles.

Brearley, M. and Hitchfield, E. *A Teacher's Guide to Reading Piaget.* London: Routledge & Kegan Paul, 1966. In the U.S. in paperback, Schocken Books, Inc.

   The authors aim to help teachers acquire a method for reading the complex work of Piaget. His work is quoted and commented on.

Inhelder, Barbel and Jean Piaget. *The Growth of Logical Thinking.* Basic Books, 1958.

   Begins with the child's thinking from seven to eleven years, the "concrete operations stage" and follows its changes through the "formal operations stage," twelve to fifteen years.

Isaacs, Susan. *Intellectual Growth in Children.* New York: Schocken Books, Inc., 1968.

   An educational classic presenting observations of children's intellectual development within practical situations.

Isaacs, Susan. *The Children We Teach: Seven to Eleven Years.* New York: Schocken Books, Inc., 1971 (first published 1932).

   Discusses the behavior and mental life of children aged seven to eleven and contains an analysis of the emotional difficulties that often lead to backwardness in reading.

Mackay, David; Thompson, Brian; and Schaub, Pamela. *Breakthrough to Literacy.* (Teacher's Manual, Children's Reading Materials). Longman's Gray, Ltd., 1970. R. R. Bowker Co., New York.

Practical assistance for teachers of primary grades who want to allow children to move into reading from their own composing and writing. Includes easy books for early stages of reading.

Marsh, Leonard. *Alongside the Child*. New York: Harper and Row, 1972.

Gives good descriptions of informal education with upper-grade children.

Schools Council (England). *Science Curriculum 5/13*. London: Macdonald Educational Publishers, 1972-73.

A series of science units for teachers (and children) which encourage investigations. The units are linked to broad objectives which children are likely to meet through their work. Titles include:
With Objectives in Mind,
Working with Wood Stages 1 and 2,
Working with Wood Background Information,
Time Stages 1 and 2,
Early Experiences,
Structures and Forces Stages 1 and 2,
Science from Toys Stages 1 and 2,
Structures and Forces Stage 3,
Minibeasts Stages 1 and 2

Silberman, Charles E. (ed.). *The Open Classroom Reader*. New York: Vintage Books, 1973.

Contains sixty-five of the best selections from American, English, and Canadian sources on informal or open education. Includes practical suggestions and detailed descriptions of activities, as well as theoretical positions.

Wadsworth, Barry J. *Piaget's Theory of Cognitive Development*. New York: David McKay Co., 1971.

Concise introduction to Piagetian stages of development with examples from Piaget.